By the SEA

Laughing Elephant

MMXIV

The beach is a wonderful place where
There is nothing to do but
Play or Relax.

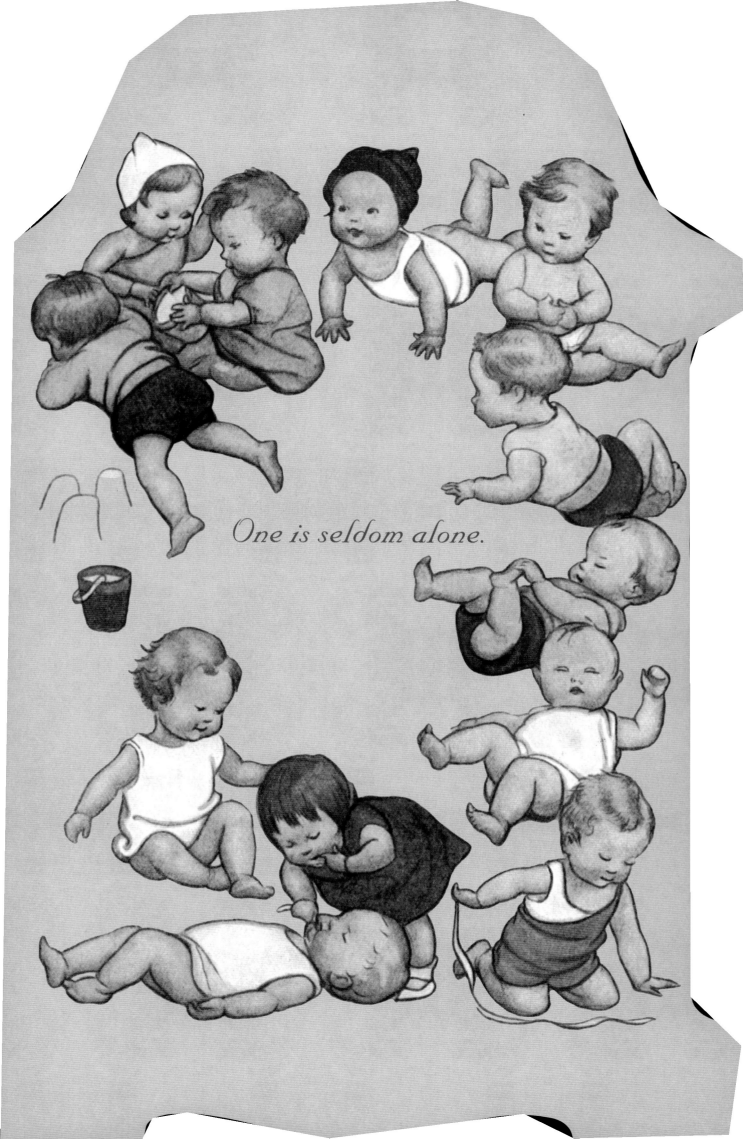

One is seldom alone.

On the beach
Everyone can build things . . .

Simple or Complicated

It's a place where
There is always something new to see,

And we are always learning

On the beach we can each
Build our own world,

And make our pretending
Come true.

There is always the wonderful water,
So fresh, delightful,

And so welcoming.

On the beach
We always meet new people,

And they often become friends.

The beach is such
A place of good times,

That even the grown-ups have fun.

We are always sad when a
Day at the beach ends,

And look forward to coming again.